Mary Cassatt
Family Pictures

by
Claire Leonard

by Jane O'Connor
illustrated by Jennifer Kalis

Grosset & Dunlap • New York

To Robby and Teddy, my favorite artists—J.O'C.
To my parents, for believing in me—J.K.

Text copyright © 2003 by Jane O'Connor. Illustrations copyright © 2003 by Jennifer Kalis. All rights reserved. Published by Grosset & Dunlap, a division of Penguin Putnam Books for Young Readers, 345 Hudson Street, New York, NY 10014. GROSSET & DUNLAP is a trademark of Penguin Putnam Inc. Published simultaneously in Canada. Manufactured in China.

Library of Congress Cataloging-in-Publication Data

O'Connor, Jane, 1947—
  Mary Cassatt : family pictures / by Jane O'Connor ; illustrated by Jennifer Kalis.
    p. cm. — (Smart about art)
Summary: Discusses the life and the work of the Impressionist painter Mary Cassatt, as told from a child's point of view.
  1. Cassatt, Mary, 1844—1926—Juvenile literature. 2. Painters—United States—Biography—Juvenile literature.
[1. Cassatt, Mary, 1844—1926. 2. Artists. 3. Women—Biography.] I. Kalis, Jennifer, ill. II. Title. III. Series.
ND237.C3O25 2003
759.13—dc21   2002151305

ISBN 0-448-43152-1 (pbk)   B C D E F G H I J
ISBN 0-448-43153-X (GB)   A B C D E F G H I J

From the desk of

Ms. Brandt

Dear Class,

Our unit on famous artists is almost over. I hope that you enjoyed it as much as I did.

I am excited to read your reports. Here are some questions that you may want to think about:

- Why did you pick your artist?

- If you could ask your artist 3 questions, what would they be?

- Did you learn anything that really surprised you?

Good luck and have fun!

Ms. Brandt

After my baby sister was born last October, our family got lots of cards congratulating us. The card below was my favorite. It shows a mother holding her baby on her shoulder. I like how the baby is hugging his mom around the neck. My sister does the same thing. From the way the mother is smiling, you know she thinks he is absolutely the world's greatest baby.

The Young Mother by Mary Cassatt. Private Collection/Christie's Images/Bridgeman Art Library.

My Sister

I like the soft colors and the peaceful, quiet feeling of the picture, although it is hardly *ever* peaceful or quiet at our house (so that part is not like real life).

It turns out that the picture was by an American artist named Mary Cassatt. She was famous for her paintings of mothers and children. I had never heard of her before, but since I liked the painting so much I decided to pick her for my report.

Mary Cassatt was nothing like I imagined. I figured that Mary Cassatt must have had children of her own. But I was wrong. She never even got married. For most of her life, she lived in France. She was great friends with the painter Edgar Degas. Some people thought she might marry him.

Here is what Mary said:

What a repulsive idea!

I thought that Mary would be a shy, gentle person. Wrong again! Mary had a bad temper and an opinion on *everything*. During dinner parties, if her guests said something she disagreed with, she'd bang her fists on the table.

mary loved fancy hats and stylish clothes.

She doesn't look like a warm and fuzzy person — does she?

Mary Cassatt, before 1900. Research material in Mary Cassatt and James McNeill Whistler 1872-1975, Archives of American Art, Smithsonian Institution.

I found this photo on the Internet. Just by looking at the picture, you can tell Mary Cassatt was smart—and stubborn. Once she made up her mind to do something, she did it. All her life there was just one thing that she wanted—to be a great artist. And that's just what she became!

The Cassatt Family

Labels (left to right): Mr. Cassatt, Mrs. Cassatt, Robert, Alexander, Lydia, Mary, Ga...

Mary was born in 1844 in Allegheny City (which is now part of Pittsburgh), Pennsylvania. Her parents were rich. When she was a little girl, the whole family went to Paris so the children could see beautiful works of art. (America did not have any great museums yet, so people had to go to Europe to see famous paintings and statues.) The Cassatts stayed in Paris for two years before coming home. Mary went to the Louvre Museum many times. Maybe that is where she first decided to become an artist.

Pittsburgh

U.S.A.

I don't feel so well

I think I am going to throw up

I think I am going to throw up again

Pari...

The trip to Paris took two weeks. Mary was seasick the whole time.

Back in the 1860s, when girls grew up, they were just supposed to get married and have children. When Mary told her father that she was going to be an artist and sell paintings for a living, he had a fit.

But later on her parents gave in and sent Mary to art school Philadelphia. After four years of classes, Mary thought she d learned all she could. She was ready to go back to Paris— thout her parents this time.

The trouble was that Paris was a hard place for young artists to get a start. Every year, there was a big art show called the Salon. If your paintings weren't in the show, it was really tough to sell them. Judges decided which paintings would be accepted. There were rules for painting—just like in spelling.

Judge

please choose mine. Pretty please! Pretty please with sugar on top!

Here are some of the Salon rules.

1. Make really big pictures— the bigger the better.

2. Paint important stuff like famous battle scenes or heroes from legends.

3. Don't let any brush strokes show.

4. Use dark colors.

This is a painting of Mary's that got into the Salon. She was very excited. But soon she decided the Salon rules were foolish. (I think she was right.) She liked the paintings that some of the younger artists in Paris were doing. The Salon never took their pictures. So these artists got together and decided to have their own show.

Hooray! The Salon liked this!

On the Balcony by Mary Cassatt. 1873. Philadelphia Museum of Art: Gift of John G. Johnson for the W. P. Wilstach Collection.

These artists were called "Impressionists" because their pictures gave an impression of the scene without putting in lots of details.

This is called "Train in the Snow". It is by Claude Monet.

Train in the Snow by Claude Monet. 1875. Musée Marmottan. Paris, France/Bridgeman Art Library.

Most people thought their art show was a joke. Nobody wanted to buy their paintings. But when these artists asked Mary to join their group, what do you think she did?

This is by
Pierre Auguste
Renoir ↳

This is by
Edgar
Degas ↓

The Luncheon of the Boating Party by Pierre Auguste Renoir. 1881. Phillips Collection. Washington DC. USA/Bridgeman Art Library.

The Laundresses by Edgar Degas. 1884. Musée d'Orsay. Paris. France/Bridgeman Art Library.

The Impressionists broke all the rules of the Salon. They liked to paint ordinary people doing ordinary stuff, like having lunch at a restaurant or ironing shirts. They painted with big, loose brush strokes; sometimes they even left part of the picture empty with the canvas showing through. They used bright colors and painted outdoors to show what grass and flowers and fields looked like in sunlight.

Portrait of the Artist by Mary Cassatt. 1878. The Metropolitan Museum of Art. Bequest of Edith H. Proskauer, 1975. (1975.319.1) Photograph © 1998 The Metropolitan Museum of Art.

Here is a painting that Mary did after she joined the group of Impressionists. You can see right away how different it is from the painting she did that the Salon liked. It is a self-portrait, a painting Mary did of herself. Mary is leaning against a sofa in a white dress and fancy hat. It looks like she painted the sofa and her dress in a hurry. You can see the big brush strokes. And Mary didn't put anything in the background. It's all a solid color.

Of all the Impressionists, Mary thought Edgar Degas was the most talented. For Mary, looking at a Degas painting was like looking at the most delicious candy.

Beware of DOGS!

Degas admired Mary's paintings, too. He thought that Mary had great talent. He even helped Mary with some of her paintings. (He may have painted the white curtains in the picture.) I know how the girl in this picture feels . . . bored and pooped.

Little Girl in a Blue Armchair by Mary Cassatt. 1878. Mellon Collection, National Gallery of Art, Washington DC, USA/Bridgeman Art Library.

The dog is one of Mary's pets. He looks worn-out too. Mary had lots of little dogs. She was crazy about them. But I read in a book that nobody else was. The dogs barked a lot and nipped at people's ankles. Kids who posed for her were scared of them. I wonder if the girl in the painting was.

woof!

woof!

woof!

Mary kept toys and candy in her studio for the children who posed for her. She knew sitting still and posing for a painting was hard work. Once her nephew got so sick of posing that he spit at her. His parents punished him. Mary felt sorry for him. So she brought him a present the next day.

This is
a painting
of Mary's
brother
and one
of her
nephews.

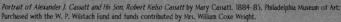

Portrait of Alexander J. Cassatt and His Son, Robert Kelso Cassatt by Mary Cassatt. 1884–85. Philadelphia Museum of Art: Purchased with the W. P. Wilstach Fund and funds contributed by Mrs. William Coxe Wright.

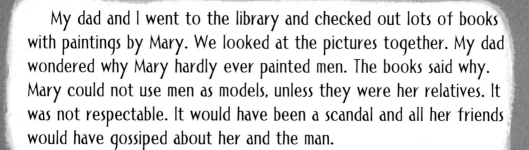

My dad and I went to the library and checked out lots of books with paintings by Mary. We looked at the pictures together. My dad wondered why Mary hardly ever painted men. The books said why. Mary could not use men as models, unless they were her relatives. It was not respectable. It would have been a scandal and all her friends would have gossiped about her and the man.

So Mary did paintings of her friends and family doing the same things she did, like going to the ballet.

DO
YOU
see
the
dancer
yawning?

The Rehearsal Onstage by Edgar Degas. 1874(?). The Metropolitan Museum of Art. H.O. Havemeyer Collection. Bequest of Mrs. H.O. Havemeyer. 1929. (29.100.39) Photograph © 1978 The Metropolitan Museum of Art.

This painting of a rehearsal is by Degas.

Edgar Degas went to the ballet all the time. He is famous for his paintings and drawings of dancers. But Degas showed what was happening on stage or backstage.

Mary was more interested in painting the audience. This lady is watching the ballet. At the top there is a man leaning over the railing. He has little binoculars, too. But he is watching her! I wonder what the story is there.

The people in the background are just squiggles and dots.

In the Loge; 1879; Mary Stevenson Cassatt American, 1844-1926; Oil on canvas 81.28 x 66.04 cm (32 x 26 in.); Museum of Fine Arts, Boston, The Hayden Collection-Charles Henry Hayden Fund; 10.35. © 2002 Museum of Fine Arts, Boston.

Daytime

Nighttime

Guess if the lady is at an afternoon show or a nighttime show. If you said "afternoon," you are right. You can tell from the way she's dressed. At night, ladies wore fancy ball gowns to the theater.

Ladies like Mary and her friends had tea parties in the afternoon. Mary did many paintings of teatime. The lady drinking tea is the guest. Guests did not take off their hats or gloves because they only stayed a little while—just long enough for a piece of cake and one cup of tea. Staying longer would have been considered rude.

↙ Lydia

The Tea: about 1880; Mary Stevenson Cassatt American, 1844-1926; Oil on canvas; 64.77 x 92.07 cm (25 1/2 x 36 1/4 in.); Museum of Fine Arts, Boston; M. Theresa B. Hopkins Fund; 42.178. © 2002 Museum of Fine Arts, Boston.

↳ Mary's tea set

The lady without the hat is Mary's sister, Lydia. To me, it looks as though she is thinking over a piece of gossip that the other lady has just told her.

Oops! I didn't
get all of my mom
in the photo.

In the late 1800s when Mary was painting, the first
snapshots were invented. In a snapshot, often some of
the picture accidentally gets cut off, like my mom's
head. Mary and the other Impressionists liked to do the
same thing in their paintings. In the tea party painting,
the fireplace and the mirror above it are cut off.
Mary shows what is most interesting—the two ladies
and her beautiful silver tea set!

Mary also painted pictures of ladies at home sewing or knitting or reading. The lady here is Mary's mother. She is in a white dress against a white wall, reading a white newspaper. But Mary made lots of different shades of white by using other colors like pink and gray and cream. If you look closely you can see them.

Lots of Mary's paintings have mirrors in them.

She liked to show reflections.

Reading Le Figaro by Mary Cassatt. 1878. Private Collection/Christie's Images/Bridgeman Art Library.

In 1877, Mary's mother and father and her sister, Lydia, came to Paris to visit. Guess what?
They never left!

Hello, dear. We've come for a short visit!

Mary went back to the U.S. only two more times. (She hated long trips on ships because she never got over her seasickness.) Still, she always was proud to be an American. It made her sad that her paintings were much more popular in France than at home.

A Young Woman Reading a Letter by Kitagawa Utamaro. 1798. The Metropolitan Museum of Art. Rogers Fund. 1914. (JP 147) Photograph © 1994 The Metropolitan Museum of Art.

Degas

←— This Japanese lady is reading a letter.

← This is Edgar Degas.

Portrait photograph of Edgar Degas. Private Collection/Roger-Viollet. Paris/Bridgeman Art Library.

In 1891, Mary went to an art show of Japanese prints in Paris. She loved them. So did Degas. They both bought lots of Japanese prints. The art show got Mary interested in making prints of her own. (Mary eventually had her own printing press.) Degas thought Mary's prints were some of the best work she ever did.

Before she died, Mary burned all of the letters Degas had written her.

Why didn't she want anyone to see them?

Were they ♥ love letters?

Nobody ♥ knows.

The *Letter* by Mary Cassatt. 1891. The Metropolitan Museum of Art. Gift of Paul J. Sachs. 1916. (16.2.9) Photograph © 1991 The Metropolitan Museum of Art.

That is Mary's desk.

Here is one of Mary's prints. With a special needle-sharp tool, Mary drew the picture on a thin sheet of copper. This is called etching, and it is very hard to do. If you make a mistake, you can't erase it. The colors are made from different color inks that are printed onto the drawing in a printing press.

It was Degas who suggested that Mary do more paintings of mothers and children. They are the paintings she is most famous for. Most of them are indoor scenes. But not this one. There is also a man in it. That is unusual for Mary, too.

The Boating Party by Mary Cassatt. 1893–94. National Gallery of Art, Washington DC, USA/Index/Bridgeman Art Library.

I finished drawing the boat.

When part of a picture is cut off, it's called cropping.

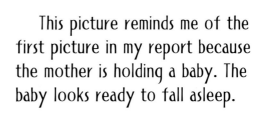

This picture reminds me of the first picture in my report because the mother is holding a baby. The baby looks ready to fall asleep.

The Young Mother by Mary Cassatt. Private Collection/Christie's Images/Bridgeman Art Library.

Look how Mary didn't bother to finish painting the print on the skirt or the baby's foot.

Mary Cassatt, American, 1844-1926, The Child's Bath, 1893, oil on canvas, 39 1/2 x 26 in., Robert A. Waller Fund. 1910.2, image © The Art Institute of Chicago.

I like all the different patterns in this painting. It's also interesting that you seem to be looking down at the mother and baby from above.

Miranda in the tub.

I have to be honest. I don't like this portrait as much as I like the other pictures. I think the little girl looks too cute, if you know what mean. I feel bad saying this, because Mary was losing her eyesight when she painted this. By the end of her life, she was almost completely blind. That is so sad, especially for an artist.

Francoise Holding A Little Dog by Mary Cassatt. 1906. The Huntington Library, Art Collections, and Botanical Gardens, San Marino, California/SuperStock.

After 1914, Mary couldn't paint anymore. She thought her paintings were pretty but not great enough to be in museums.

She was wrong! We took a trip to New York City and at the Metropolitan Museum of Art I saw six paintings by Mary. It was amazing to be up so close to them! Sometimes the colors were very different from the way they looked in my books. And in books, paintings always look completely flat. But I could see thick swirls and dots of paint Mary had made with her brush.

↑
I saved my buttons from the Metropolitan Museum

One of Mary's paintings of a mother and child is in the White House.

At the Metropolitan, I also saw many Impressionist paintings. When Mary's rich friends from America visited her, she got them to buy lots of Impressionist paintings. (That was really nice of her because many of the Impressionists were very poor.) Years later, Mary's American friends gave their paintings to museums like the Met. Mary would be happy to know she helped American museums have great art.

My Favorite Painting

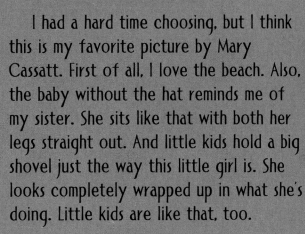

Miranda and me

I had a hard time choosing, but I think this is my favorite picture by Mary Cassatt. First of all, I love the beach. Also, the baby without the hat reminds me of my sister. She sits like that with both her legs straight out. And little kids hold a big shovel just the way this little girl is. She looks completely wrapped up in what she's doing. Little kids are like that, too.

My Three Questions

If I got to meet Mary Cassatt, here's what I would ask her:

1. Why are the people in your pictures always sitting down?
2. Were you and Edgar Degas in love?
3. How come you destroyed all the artwork you did as a young student?

And I bet I know what Mary would say.

None of your business.

Claire, you did a great job. I like how you imagine that there's a story going on in many of Mary Cassatt's paintings. That is what makes her pictures very interesting — the relationships between people.

Ms. Brandt